BOA
EDITIONS
LIMITED

We Didn't Come Here for This

A Memoir in Poetry by
WILLIAM B. PATRICK

ↄ

Introduction by
FRED CHAPPELL

BOA Editions, Ltd. ↄ Rochester, NY ↄ 1999

LC #: 98–71252
ISBN: 1–880238–71–3 paper

First Edition
99 00 01 02   7 6 5 4 3 2 1

Publications by BOA Editions, Ltd.—
a not-for-profit corporation under section 501 (c) (3)
of the United States Internal Revenue Code—
are made possible with the assistance of grants from
the Literature Program of the New York State Council on the Arts,
the Literature Program of the National Endowment for the Arts,
the Lannan Foundation, the Sonia Raiziss Giop Charitable Foundation,
the Eric Mathieu King Fund of The Academy of American Poets,
as well as from the Mary S. Mulligan Charitable Trust,
the County of Monroe, NY,
and from many individual supporters.

Cover Design: Nancy David
Typesetting: Richard Foerster
Manufacturing: McNaughton & Gunn, Lithographers
BOA Logo: Mirko

Contents

❧

A memoir is how one remembers
one's own life.
—Gore Vidal

The Level Gaze of William B. Patrick

Jim and Betty were married in 1946. He had just returned from the harrowing experiences of the war; she was a modest, inexperienced Catholic girl. Their first son, Jimmy, was born in 1947. Billy, who hears and reports these poems, was born in 1949. Three other children followed: Tommy in 1951, David in 1954, and Steven in 1958. Tommy died as an infant, and David was afflicted with cerebral palsy.

And that's it—that is the whole exterior chronicle outlined by William B. Patrick's sinewy sequence of poems, *We Didn't Come Here for This*. It is a sad story in many ways, yet it is reported, by participants as well as by poet, as being nothing unusual, nothing remarkable. In a book glinting with wry humor, one of the wryest moments occurs when the thirteen-year-old Billy meets the film star Jayne Mansfield in the succulent flesh, and compares his gritty situation to what he imagines to be her supralunary one: "I wonder if Jayne Mansfield even thinks about / ordinary people like us."

It is this insistence on ordinariness that gives William Patrick's work its vehement muscularity. If the story is sad, still it is not tragic in the poet's view, and he does not attempt to inflate it to an Aeschylean or Shakespearean level. If the characters are stricken or perplexed or furious, they are still not Cassandra nor Hamlet nor Lear. I have the strong impression that the poet believes treating Betty, Jim, Tommy, and David as grand tragic figures would be rude effrontery, an assault on their personal integrity—an insult to his own.

Personal integrity is not only a quality but a concept central to William Patrick's work. All poets must be concerned with it, but they generally appeal to it as a corrective, as a means of testing for any falsity that might have slipped through the processes of writing and censoring and onto the page. But Patrick finds for it a more aggressive employment: certain materials present themselves to him and their aspect is, at first glance, truculent, common, even drab. These are merely the facts of the case and the task he discovers is not to prettify them into verse but to denude them into poetry. Wallace Stevens declared that poetry must evade the pressure of reality; I can easily picture with what a skeptical grin William Patrick would greet that pronouncement.

We Didn't Come Here for This is poetry, of course it is; but it is poetry on its own terms, a kind of utterance that does not borrow from books the sometimes stilted magnificence of traditional literature or the sometimes exhibitionist quirkiness of contemporary writing. On a vacation trip to Florida with his family after Tommy's death, the young Billy is granted a vision of his brother singing to him from a lucent pool-bottom, inviting him to join him in the lovely submarine afterlife the departed one now enjoys. But when he tries to join his brother, he is saved from drowning in brutal fashion: "My mother holds my face and cries. 'Stupid / bastard,' my father shouts down at me. 'Jesus / Christ, we didn't come here for this, you know.'"

Here and everywhere the impulse toward an elevated tragic tone is undercut by the petty cruelties of everyday life. The father, unable to talk with his wife about the loss of their son, Tommy, parades the information to a customer as part of his pitch as a car salesman: "What the hell, you can't pick the family / you land in, right? Let me tell you, thank God none of your kids / has died." The father is one of those who can see himself only as being a victim.

For example, even with Jim's own father, Billy's grandfather, laid out at a funeral home, he retains his power to bully and frighten. When told to view his grandfather's body, Billy "jumped up like his clothes were on fire and ran straight out / Mason's front door, / out onto 109th Street. He tore up toward Oakwood Cemetery / and made it across 6th Avenue, / onto the boulevard strip of grass, before I caught up with him. / What the hell, Dad, / you figured out how to scare / everybody. At least I learned that—Billy was scared to death when I grabbed him."

The integrity that saves William Patrick from the overblown phrase, the histrionic attitude, the pompous gesture, also provides him with what Ernest Hemingway called the "built-in shit detector." Sentimentality cannot enter here; the characters may invite and feed upon guilt feelings or they may make excuses for themselves, but the poet will have none of it. Jim's horrendous war experiences did not cause his fatherly violence toward his family; the loss of Tommy does not justify Betty's withdrawal from her marriage; the grandfather's abuse of his wife and son is no excuse for the father's cool and dangerous fecklessness. No, each person is responsible for what he or she does and is, and the situation that results is no more than the sum of the facts of the case.

The facts, though, are complicated, for if the destinies reported here are ordinary, still it is important to fit them into some larger framework. "October 3, 1949, 7:08 A.M." is a humorous (and melancholy) attempt to attain an overview, to place the life of this family in cosmic and historical context. The poet imagines his soul, on the day of his birth, coming from Elsewhere to inhabit his body on earth, skimming along the handle of the Big Dipper, meandering through Draco, sailing down over Mongolia to Communist China and Russia, then to America and the Garden State, where it passes up the chance to become Bruce Springsteen. Then it travels north over Yankee Stadium and on to Albany and Troy, passing Jacob Lindy's soul as it sails up from the Fivels' house on Hoosick Road, where the poet's soul "heard my mother's mother praying / for her unborn/ godson / another William / named for her William Howard / the husband she would never stop loving;" and finally the soul "pulled on its gloves / with the empty fingers / and throttled back / for a flawless / one-point / landing" and became—ta-da!—William Patrick, author of *Letter to the Ghosts*, *Roxa: Voices of the Culver Family*, *These Upraised Hands*, and *We Didn't Come Here for This*.

That was a miracle, of course, but still nothing unusual, only one of the facts of the case—though it is the fact that made the recording of the other facts possible. And if these facts are not remarkable, still they have urgency, whether Jayne Mansfield understands it or not. Maybe, just maybe, in the broadest scheme of things, this regular family, "where kids die / and can't walk right / and people yell at each other a lot," can assume as much importance as the career of a mountainously glamorous movie star. Maybe someone should tell Jayne that: maybe *We Didn't Come Here for This* does tell her. I hear it speaking to me, anyhow, in a voice easy and open, almost casual in tone, and with a level, earnest honesty, saying that, yes, these events are "regular" not extraordinary in the least—but as important as sunlight.

Fred Chappell

JIM AND BETTY IN THE YARD AT WATERFORD, NY, EASTER, 1946

If there had been even one torpedo-shaped cloud
                              in this perfect sky,
                                        one cloud,
or if Betty's dog, Yehudi—that she called "Hootie"
                    and who mushrooms here behind Jim
                                        along this photo's right edge,
            like a shell-shocked evergreen shrub—
if Hootie had chosen this carefully posed moment to squat
                    and alter the crystalline air,
            or if the cropped grass
                              were simply wet,
so the engaged couple found themselves standing,
            the war hero
                        shifting weight off his scarred leg
      to lean away from her already,
                        the young Catholic socialite
                  clutching her white purse
                  in front of her saved
                        virginity,
then one of these postwar lovebirds, my parents-to-be,
            gazing at themselves afterward,
                              might have thought twice.

                  But why,
sitting here so striking and young in their still-buttoned Easter suits,
                  smiling,
            centered and framed
                        in her parents' sunlit backyard
            by what lies ahead,
      like a pair of mallards on their first spring migration,
                  should they?
      What could go wrong, for them, here, in 1946?
Workers at GM had won their wage hike,
            Betty's dad would sell more Chevies,

the Thoroughbreds would enchant
another Saratoga August,
and the white pickets that guard the bright horizon here, border to border,
behind these budding poplars,
would keep Mr. Kelts's goats out of their perfect tomatoes
one more season.
A corsage of orchids spills from her right shoulder and stops at her breast.
His left knee is drawn up, showing a snug argyle,
two bands of light and one dark with a tipped
X
in the middle,
a white cross under his yawning cuff.
Jim rests his arm on that knee and leans his right shoulder against her,
showing his good intentions,
and his head is only a few pickets away from Betty's hair.
But for all that
there is still something wrong.
The sun, high up,
from the right,
coaxes half of each face into shadow,
and I can—
wherever I am then,
near some temporary heaven, perhaps, waiting to be again—
I can see them.
Somehow I hear them thinking.

*It was D-Day plus 8 when Charlie Dunlap
stole the Calvados—two jugs of it.
Real rotgut, rip your throat out when
you took it down. Six of us—all
Rangers, Company A—were sent to
stop the Kraut officers, the bastards
trying to reach Brest, where they
had submarine pens . . . and we
couldn't FIND Charlie. The country
women were washing their clothes,
slapping them on rocks in the river.
What the hell RIVER was that? . . . So
that's where Charlie was—spread-
eagled, half in the water, completely*

cock-eyed, laughing—I mean he was
shot in the ass, absolutely blotto,
watching those peasant broads wash
their drawers.

Daddy said,
"Just pick somebody I won't have to stick
on the washrack. Somebody with brains."
Daddy sells 2,000 cars a year,
and Jim has enough brains to take over there,
enough to be somebody.
Last summer, at the country club,
Jim was home on leave, in his uniform, et cetera.
His mom called me over.
Our first date was golf. He always wants to
play golf, and I'm not a golfer,
so what will we do about that?
I was terrible and he was great,
but he's so good at everything.
Anyway we played, and he still asked me out,
even after that.
I keep thinking about Freddie Schwartz.
He is eight years older.
I like that.
And he was a glider pilot. He went over and fought.
I thought he was the love of my life.

Where do we float
between our lives?
Why do we choose the ones
who help us back?

So we hauled Charlie up the riverbank
and moved out. Then two things
happened. We came to this town,
behind their lines—ours were WAY the hell
back. So the people went nuts, jumping
around, grabbing us, yelling in French,
THE WAR'S OVER,
THE AMERICANS ARE HERE,

and this baker and his daughter, young,
like 16 or 17, run out with hot bread,
with butter already on it. She grabs my
shoulders, looks up into my eyes and
bang-o, plants the goddamnedest lip-lock
on me, and then pushes some buttered
bread IN MY MOUTH. Jesus, I couldn't get her
out of my head . . . right up till the next day,
when we mined the Brest road
and caught that truckload of Nazis.

I wonder if Freddie would have
asked me to marry him.
He's so handsome
at the Ten Eyck tea dances,
so thin and sophisticated, et cetera.
Not jitterbuggy with you where you're always
flying around. I'm not good at that.
But he doesn't have potential,
not like Jim.
Freddie lives in a third-floor walk-up
with his father, who's a lawyer.
I can't hitch my star to Freddie.
Jim's more of a go-getter.

Then this French kid—looked about
twelve years old, for Chrissakes—tells us
some Jerries, some officers, are having
a picnic over at his farm . . . What the HELL
did we follow him back for? No sooner
do we swing open the gate and all step
inside but they slam us—little son
of a bitch led us into a trap. We lost
two guys, fought our way out. The Krauts
took off up through an orchard, and after
it was done we found that collaborator kid.
Charlie Dunlap got that LOOK of his . . .
He dragged the kid out to the back, kicking
him the whole way, laughing like when he
was back shit-faced with those broads at the

river. The kid had these eyes like—I don't
KNOW what . . . I want to FORGET what they
were is all . . . Then Charlie threw the kid
inside his own woodshed, with all these wooden
rakes and rusted tools hanging on hooks—
it looked just like my father's woodshed
out behind our kitchen where he used
that goddamn leather whip with the strips
ON ME—and then Charlie shot him.

Jim gave me the engagement ring
on St. Valentine's Day.
I never expected that.
I found out later he bought it
the day I was skiing with Freddie.
Anyway, it was fun.
We were at dinner, at Keeler's.
He wrote a poem to go with it.
I know it now, by heart.
The first half goes,

> "I'd have to be a great Romancer,
> To know the nature of your answer,
> So for weeks I've been in a fret,
> Not knowing what to expect;"

and then,

> "We've kidded and kissed,
> And had a great time;
> So here's *your* valentine,
> With a question, 'Will you be mine?'"

It was bad. I saw how scared the kid was.
I could have said, I don't know, "Charlie,
let's go," or . . . I could feel that kid
like he was breathing INSIDE of me, feel
him just aching to stay alive, but then
Charlie sprayed him, up and down, fast,
with his Thompson. It was BAD. The kid
exploded on us. We were upset, but there
were bodies everywhere . . . Later on,

we went back through that baker's town—
God, I wanted to screw that girl—what
would Betty think of THAT? They told
us that same kid ratted on the baker
and his daughter, to the Nazis, for giving us
the buttered bread. The Kraut bastards
stuck both of them in their own oven
and burned them up. I sat down right there
and cried—for her, but for missing a chance
at her, too—what the hell DIFFERENCE does
any of it make? I can see her eyes now
in front of me, and I can still hear Charlie
laughing about that kid in the woodshed.

It's a solitaire diamond.
It's so lovely,
and I was truly surprised.
Jim is a go-getter.
I know it.
Freddie doesn't have that
whatever it is
that Jim has.
Determination, maybe.
When we saw Notorious *last week,*
I kept watching Cary Grant
as he kissed Ingrid Bergman,
and that's how Jim looks,
the way he leans in, and hesitates,
that determined look he gets,
as he's staring down at me.

I should leave them alone here,
and not want to return so much.
They love each other.
They're happy here.
What will happen to them later
doesn't matter.
I should find another way to start again,
but there is

something here,
something I must need,
something in their relentless shadows that keeps me locked
on these two.
Just look.

No one can warn
either of them about the other.
They're too happy to listen.
It's perfect.

A Wedding Candid Arrives for Betty

November 8, 1947

Dear Clara,

What is wrong with me?
I've been crying, just twisting my ring
since they took Jimmy back to the nursery,
since I propped his bottle up for him—about the only thing
they let me do, thank God—and now my finger's started to bleed.
It's silly to sound helpless, but I feel stupid
lying here, staring out at clouds all day long.
What else is there? I'll be stuck in here
ten days. No, eleven, when you add
the first day's labor.
I am just so bad

with babies. You know.
We never baby-sat. Tell me where
we'd find kids in the Depression? There *were* no
kids, remember? And I was an only child. No other
babies but me. So when the nurse brings him, at 2, 6 & 10
each day, I panic. I don't have the slightest notion
what I'm supposed to do. I feel safer
when Jimmy's not with me. It's scary
to have this tiny, live thing alone
in here. What if he
starts to choke and then

the nurse doesn't hear
my scream? At least it's not the night nurse.
She hates me. She was on during my labor
that horrible first night. "Stop crying," she said. "Your howling hurts
my ears." How could I not cry? And what a thing for her to say,
then. The doctor came and gave me ether, finally,
so I was completely out during the worst.
I had a nightmare just past midnight,

though, last night, that also made me cry.
I wasn't quiet,
and was terrified,

first, that she'd run in
and yell, but more that I'd slip back to sleep,
to the dream. Did you ever see Bones Whalen?
He was a Waterford bum my father knew. Sometimes he'd stop
at our house for food. In my dream, Bones held Jimmy by the head
over a water-trap, the kind Daddy used to set
in our barn for rats. I was pregnant still, strapped
to a metal bed near the feed-bin.
A terrible, shiny rat floated
round and round the rim.
I could hear, outside,

my father saying,
"Saw my shoes downtown, on Bones Whalen,"
over and over, and my mother laughing,
answering, "A well-dressed man wears his wing tips in a soup line."
"Let's make soup, Betty. I know exactly what we're gonna need,"
Bones said then. Jimmy's head looked battered, all smeared with blood.
"Thousand bucks and you can have him back again."
Bones grinned and swung Jimmy by one leg
over the water. "Wait, please," I said,
and I tried to dig
down, under the bed

for the money there,
but I couldn't move. "Too late," yelled Bones,
and he disappeared down into the water
with Jimmy. I woke up screaming, and a different nurse ran in,
and put her arm around me. I sound crazy, don't I? I wish
we were ten years old again, Clara, and we could watch
the band at Riley's Lake House. Helen Morgan
would sing, "My Bill," and buy fancy dolls
from those cigarette girls for each
of us. We were all
happy then. I wish

another woman—
a friend, I guess—could be with me. Here.
Thanks for the candid wedding photo you sent.
Jim looks so puzzled in it, and so small, clutching your flowers.
And mother's face, too, as her hand is swallowed by your bouquet,
seems sad, because I picked out a Protestant, maybe,
and we couldn't be married at the altar.
I look so angry in this picture,
as if I'm getting ready to leave.
So close to that door.
If you could see me,

lying here still fat—
what's gone wrong with me? Jim's playing golf
every weekend now, and working day and night,
lugging typewriters all over for his miserable oaf
of a father, who gambles away our commission money.
Sorry. I'm just really terrified of the baby,
Clara. I keep worrying, asking myself
which life is real—before, or now.
And last night, why did I have that dream?
Jim's love's real, though,
right? Please write to me.
                                        Betty

Jim and Jimmy at 304 Hoosick Street, Troy, June 1948

Some things you can't explain to women. "He's afraid,"
                 Betty hollered, a couple of times,
before I set her straight—"I let you baptize him," I yelled back.
                 "Now let ME teach him what I want."
Jimmy wouldn't quit squirming and screaming and just sit there
                 in his tub. And I was going slow,
too, lowered his feet in a little bit, splashed some on his belly . . .
                 "He's a baby. He's afraid of the water"—
"JESUS, that's the point. What is there to be afraid OF here?
                 No boy named after me will be afraid."
James Knox Patrick the third, named after me, me after my father,
                 and him after his uncle, born on the day
James Knox Polk was inaugurated our eleventh President—
                 fourth day of March, 1845.
Jimmy cried when the priest spilled the holy water on his head,
                 and nobody hollered at HIM.
You have to edge fear out early, and substitute toughness.
                 I was scared to death of my father,
because I knew how tough he was. He had only half a right foot,
                 and he suffered that his whole life.
He grew up in Mechanicville, and had to catch a train to Albany,
                 to get to college down there.
Well, one morning, in winter, he had a nosebleed and was late.
                 He jumped at the last train car,
missed, and it took off his foot. Squared his shoe straight across.
                 The doctors couldn't sew it back on,
not in 1913, so they stitched the skin over and left him a STUMP.
                 And he wore a stump sock,
heavy fabric to cover the wound, pulled all the way up to the knee.
                 But here's how tough he was—
the stump sock rubbed against an artificial foot made of leather
                 every time he took a step.
For twenty years, the front of that stump never healed.
                 He walked on an OPEN sore.

And every morning, my mother had to lay a new dressing on it.
              "Fixing his foot," she called it.
She took Balsam Peru, spread it on gauze, and then taped that,
              both ways, to cover the wound.
In winter, she held the bottle with pliers above the gas flame
              to coax it out of the bottle.
If it weren't for bowling, he'd be walking on that open sore STILL.
              In 1933 my mother
went to a tournament, the ABC, in California. She drove all the way
              with four other women,
and told me I had to fix my father's foot. But when the cat's away,
              you know, and the first morning
he was hungover, and it was cold. We lived at 111 2nd Avenue,
              right on the Hudson River.
Our backyard in February WAS the frozen water, and the wind
              tore across something wicked.
Our bedrooms faced out back, and the Balsam Peru was frozen.
              "Get out of here," he said.
"I got to do it. Mother'll kill me," I said. "Get lost, or I'll kill you."
              Two weeks we didn't TOUCH
his foot, and you know what happened? It SCABBED OVER.
              She was keeping it soft
with the salve, cleaning out the bacteria it needed,
              and it couldn't heal itself.
Some things you just can't explain to women, no matter what.
              She was mad as hell
at ME when she got home, even after she saw it was better.
              My father—he was BIG,
six feet and 210 at least, like his father, who they called
              the strongest man in Mechanicville.
When he worked for the railroad, the story went that he once lifted
              the two wheels and axle
of a railroad car, 2000 pounds, a couple of inches off the ground.
              But MY father beat my mother,
knelt on her shoulders, punched her in the face, even with me
              grabbing at him and shouting,
lots of times. Maybe, with that salve, she WANTED to slow him down.
              After the foot, he got ulcers,
and they made him even meaner. He used a cat-o'-nine-tails on me.
              It was wood, with leather strips,

and it hung on a nail in the kitchen—to be pointed over at,
                or taken down and SWUNG.
My first memory of him using it was at Christmastime.
                I was little, like three,
and they were gone, he and my mother, to some party somewhere.
                They left me with a baby-sitter.
So I grabbed a limb and pulled down our Christmas tree. Busted all
                my mother's lovely ornaments.
I guess the babysitter didn't grab me soon enough. I'll never forget,
                when my father came home,
and got down the cat-o'-nine-tails . . . That's the first, strong
                memory I have of him.
But I don't blame him. My father's meanness saved my life.
                When I was eight,
I walked up to 103rd Street, where the houses turned to fields.
                A set of stone stairs
led down to the river there. I found a rowboat, unhooked it,
                and rowed out where the current
rushed down toward the Ford Motor dam at Bond Street.
                Somebody spotted me pretty quick,
and the cops reached me in a boat. But my father wasn't there.
                He had them haul me away,
up to the police station in North Troy, and put me in a cell.
                Jesus, I was terrified THEN.
He came up after a few hours, and they took me in front of a judge.
                "What should I do with him?"
my father asked the judge, and he said, "Take him home now,
                but if he GOES on that river,
bring him back. We'll throw him back in the cell and lose the key."
                Then he dragged me home
and took down the cat-o'-nine-tails again. He was clever. He was.
                I didn't go near that river.
And I could feel those cops' eyes burning a hole right in my back,
                whenever I was outdoors.
MY first son. I love you. I know what I want for you.
                But you have to be tough, YOURSELF.
The world is what it is. We can't wish away all the trouble.
                I wish I could go back
and YELL to that train conductor, have him hold the morning train
                for one extra minute,

or have my baby-sitter catch that goddamned Christmas tree,
                    but I know I can't
do either one. We're all bound to get hurt, THAT'S the truth of it.
                    Your mother grew up rich,
in a warm house for the winter. She wants it all to be easy.
                    But I know better.

October 3, 1949, 7:08 A.M.

What if my soul
or whatever luminescent, immutable something
I want to believe is
my soul was
before me
set adrift like sunlight
radiant
separate from any single form
until the tethered
instant
of my birth?
To whom did it wave good-bye when
it left
to find me?
Did it start a little early
ping-pong a few light-years around the universe
skim along
Ursa Major's jagged handle
meander
through Draco
from tail to fiery head
toward Cygnus and the cold calm of black wings
forgetting flesh
worried
about nothing
out on its impeccable own
until
some signal forced memory
and it slowed for our familiar solar system?
Or
was it simply between assignments
on R and R
risen temporarily
and hovering in the bright inner ring of Saturn
watching
the ten moons

glow and darken in turn
widening its transcendental lens whenever a shooting star
flashed past?
How long
did it monitor the Earth
checking
its starry watch once in a while
measuring
what remained
of its bodiless furlough?
Down here
a light wind moved over Mongolia
toward Communist China
dragging bits of fallout from Russia's first
surprising
atomic explosion.
A hurricane
slammed into Galveston;
UMW miners on strike
in Pikeville,
Tennessee
were ambushed as they walked toward
a non-union mine;
sixteen people
died
in Ontario, California
when the Union Pacific's Pony Express train rammed
like a giant rocket
through an Air Force recreation bus
scattering soldiers
and their girls along a mile of twisted track;
and in Troy
Jacob Lindy
a well-known dairy farmer and cattle dealer
passed away
during a pleasant visit
at the home of Mr. & Mrs. Fivel on Hoosick Road
the new song
"Riders in the Sky"
leaping

from their Philco
as he crumpled over from a heart attack.
Waiting
out there
did my soul have any doubts?
Maybe
on its way down
it tried to remember
how to take everything in stride
measure out the tragic then weigh in the good
and shake all of it well.
After all
coming in over the ocean
first it got to see
Tommy Henrich catch Birdie Tebbits foul ball
and put the Yankees
into the Series
against the Brooklyn Dodgers
and then Donna Lemire
a two-year-old
who tumbled out her third-story window in Yonkers
and landed
face-down on her rag doll
wake up from her eighteen-day coma and smile.
As my soul passed over Albany
it could clearly overhear
Mildred Swanson
crooning
"Diamonds Are a Girl's Best Friend"
as she removed
permanently
her regular Sunday client's facial hair
next door to
323 Lancaster
where *an unidentified bird* dropped
a lit cigarette into
its nest
setting the whole house ablaze
so the boy
inside

printing his Science homework
FISH DO NOT SLEEP
THEY REST BY REMAINING QUIET
IN STILL POOLS
had to race out in white socks and underpants.
Maybe
when it saw Troy
my soul recalled
how it passed up the chance
at Bruce Springsteen
born
in the Garden State two weeks earlier
and as it slowed and felt
the air
52 degrees at seven-oh-eight that clear October morning
perhaps
it let
a brief pang of regret wash over.
But what if
right then
it heard my mother's mother praying
for her unborn
godson
another William
named for her William Howard
the husband she would never stop loving
and it saw my mother
pushing again
for someone else's breath
just as Jacob Lindy's soul sailed past
fluttering
like a runaway sheet
on its way up
and my soul
spiraling down
spinning
all of a sudden
almost out of control
laughing
like a maniac

ecstasy burning in its grateful eyes
one more time
pulled on its gloves
with the empty fingers
and throttled back
for a flawless
one-point
landing

.

CHRISTMAS, 1950

My father's mouth is
under the white beard with strings
that I can pull down.

My face, laughing, looks
up from one shiny snowboot
and then the other.

Don't touch Jimmy's dog.
Don't. Or his new firehouse. No,
don't, or he'll hit you.

I see light, like stars,
like music sparking, bouncing
off the bright, new snow.

If the baby duck
walks fast on my new barn roof,
his mother will yell.

The red birds land on
snowy branches. My red cup
of milk hits the floor.

My Christmas tree smells.
The tinsel tastes like doorknobs.
The needles bite you.

The brown bird outside
sees his friends clipped to the tree,
and wants to come in.

The gray Fairbanks truck
brings the wind to Hoosick Street,
turning the spruce blue.

My father wears red
pants, red coat, a red hat, and
stands by our fireplace.

I push my rocking
chair next to my brother's chair,
but sometimes he moves.

Some of the white clouds
carry angels who can see
from God down to me.

The empty branches
of the crab-apple tree don't
catch the broken clouds.

I can't wear Jimmy's
hat. Babies can't be cowboys
until they turn three.

My father's wires
hold the tree tight in water
so it doesn't die.

When my father plays
a record, my mother laughs.
I see all her teeth.

The red ornament
makes me big, but curves the couch
tall around my head.

Jimmy puts my cows
inside his long, silver truck
and takes them away.

My grandmother's hands
want the cookies to be trees,
and stars, and houses.

Lay this green blanket
over my barn, fence, pigs, horse,
cows, sheep. Keep them warm.

The way snow floats down,
thinking of where it came from,
telling me to sleep.

A Family Picnic on an Island in Lake George, July 1951

The small boy wearing a life vest
stands on a shadowy rock near the lake-edge.
Sunlight washes part of the water white.
He can hear the perch behind him
tracing circles in the close water,
holding colored pencils in their mouths,
but they swallow them when he turns to watch.
His brother's face is dark with freckles,
brown like the spotted bird so hungry
in the scraggly cedar branches it can sing
only one note, *me me me me me me,*
and dark like his father's large arm
wagging the long fork at his mother.
His father shouts, *What more do you want?*
The noisy smoke coils under the hot dogs,
then wiggles out and jumps toward the sky.
It's not just the golf, his mother says,
scraping butter on the white rolls, rolling
her red shoulders down, the way she stands
to dress each morning in her deep closet
where the boy is too afraid to look. *You're never
here even when you're here,* she says.
*I skipped the tournament. I'm here. We have
the boat.* The kid on the *Saturday Post*
cover looks like his brother, but with hair
a longer orange, and the doctor's hairy hand
holds a black circle on his chest, but now
his brother rolls the doctor and kid
into a paper stick and smashes a fly.
The small boy is afraid of doctors.
Once his mother pushed him onto the red couch
and the doctor tugged his pants down
for the shiny needle. *You're never really here,*
he hears his mother say another time.

Now the boy does a flip backward
into the lake, sinks to the dark bottom,
and sits there. One perch coloring another's
orange stripes nods and smiles at the boy.
Two snails are in a fierce race
around a green Coke bottle half-filled
with mud. A rainbow trout is humming
a tune the boy has heard his father sing—
*Good morning, Mr. Zip, Zip, Zip, with your hair
cut just as short as mine. Good morning,
Mr. Zip, Zip, Zip, you're really looking fine.*
Suddenly, his mother's arms hurry
into the water above him. Words bubble out of her
fingers: *I have another baby inside me,*
words that disappear when the boy sees them
like the corkscrew clams that rock shut
inside the mud, or the birthday balloons
that exploded in his brother's hands.
God gave us another baby, his mother
had told him. Now his father dives in beside him
and slits open a sunfish with his thumbnail.
Fish have babies, too. His father opens the cut
and shiny marbles full of fish-eyes tumble out
and roll up toward sunlight at the water's top.
The boy can hear the wind moving shadows
out of the crowded tree limbs on the mountain
above him. He can follow an arrow of light
the sun fires across the shifting water.
His father is squeezing the sunfish belly red
and his mother's hands bounce clamshells
back and forth like muddy castanets.
The boy wants the perch to color his hair
an orange like his brother's, like his father's,
so everyone will stop yelling at him.
He wants to ask this father next to him
who God is and how He gives babies
to mothers. He wants to ask his mother's hands
how to see angels when they fly,
but the sunlight is so loud on the water
he wouldn't hear their answers. *I know,*

he thinks, and he floats up onto the rock
again. With a borrowed pencil,
he draws his parents on the stone,
his mother's small hand curled
inside his father's fist, and he gives them
wings, curved and white and longer than both
of them standing on tiptoe,
and he lets them fly.

The Night of Tommy's Funeral Betty
Talks about His Death, November 11, 1952

What do we want what's left after I don't know now—tell me, anybody,
what are we supposed to feel, actually, when what's left is this,
is some messed-up photograph?

Look at this here, look, on the left, by Tommy's right arm they can't even
do this one thing—just leave him plain, okay, however he was
the week before, like this on Jimmy's

birthday, November 4. It was warm enough some robins—enough they
could wear the new clothes we bought at Saks, as if, maybe I knew
it was too cold under here on

Tommy's legs. Look at his face, he was a strong eater even hot that last
morning so sick with that 106 temperature but that was later, not
here in this picture with—whatever this

arm of light is, reaching for him. I'm a good Catholic, this doesn't mean
anything, a mistake of light not his soul ready to go for God's sake
but the camera people, I mean, ruined it.

"Stop," I told Jim, "I don't care, it's my baby, they can wait." This morning that
line of black cars stopped at the camera store, for this, at least I had
this to stand with at Tommy's grave,

to hold there. He was perfectly healthy, sick the way babies get, until over
the weekend, when Allen Totty went away—Dr. Werlin was on, he said,
"It's probably teeth. Give him aspirin,"

and I did oh God I did every three hours what the bottle said what he said.
Dr. Werlin, he was covering, "Oh, it's probably teeth," but it was a virus,
after the autopsy they called it

a virus. What do they know? "We're not really sure," they said, but a knife
        starting in—where I kissed him, to find out what why he was dead but
                do they see, after that, my baby

still? "No one particular thing," they said I couldn't hear any more—a baby,
        how could Werlin how could he not come over, Jesus Christ a baby is
                tiny, and it's so fast when you let, no

he wasn't cutting teeth not all Sunday night crying so loud I went downstairs
        so, Jimmy and Billy are little too they might without sleep, anything
                could happen but Tommy it was just

a cold, he got colds I knew them but Sunday night I went down and Jim he
        stayed the entire night upstairs. I wheeled Tommy's carriage up and
                back, singing, shushing him by the stairs

thinking maybe it didn't seem so bad morning would come soon—but right
        then I should have gone up, the second he started the what is it the
                hyperventilating so he pushed his bottle

down, I should have wakened Jim. Maybe if I . . . "Let's go," he would have said,
        no talk, just get it done, hurry now, the emergency room, don't wait
                for someone else, for your Dr. Totty,

for morning. I held Tommy up watching his lips the hard breathing, I held
        his face so hot his little hand dancing around shushing him humming
                that "Singin' in the Rain" song.

He liked that he stopped crying he smiled he stared up at me singing. Maybe
        that's why I didn't—oh if I right then and they started the antibiotics
                earlier he wouldn't have, he'd be

home now. Jim's work he needs sleep, he heard the doctor was coming he left
        for work he is so busy every night late so tired but when Allen Totty
                said, "Bring Tommy to the hospital immediately,"

Jim had to leave work come up he did do that to St. Mary's. All day we sat
        there going in taking turns, he did do that to see how Tommy was and
                he was better they told us, so we went home.

We went home and slept as if we could let him be somebody else's baby like
        sleep was okay that we could forget with Kathy Bouton there, I went to
            school with her, she was his nurse but

Dr. Totty called when it was dark still out. He said it was bad we went Jim
        was with me then and we sat again with the 106 not budging until in—
            in the afternoon they came out.

Tommy was inside his little tent the plastic tent for oxygen so cloudy from
        all of his everything they, and Kathy took my hand, from school I
            remembered then she was so sweet

to me. "We did everything we could. Oxygen. Antibiotics. With a virus . . ."
        we were crying both of us but Jim kept talking to them like they—we
            had lots of help, Betty Helm

took the boys out on her day off so they could remember Tommy alive like
        in this picture. No money she wouldn't take it went to lunch the Abbott
            and Costello movie at the Bijou

and Billy laughed at first telling me how they got lost in Alaska then he cried
        he couldn't stop crying. We were home waiting for them you can't, with
            little kids, carry on like madmen,

"Tommy was just too sick to come home," I told them, "he went to heaven," but
        didn't dwell on it you have to go on living for them and what good can
            ever come talking about earlier?

I have this picture with a piece of light that won't mean anything whatever
        anyone says you can't go on believing people what they say but
            I don't know what would happen

if someday I went, where, on a ski trip maybe someplace I wouldn't be and
        all of us Jimmy Billy Jim we were all skiing, and I fell alone not hard
            but I lost my ski or something, and a young boy

stopped, a boy maybe fifteen who helped me up and I might feel he was not
        him then, not who he was in that second with sunlight but somebody I
            knew, somebody I used to know.

On Vacation with Betty's Parents, February 1953

No one knows I can find Tommy in Florida.
My mother can't hear him calling to me.

> My father came here to catch fish and smoke.
> He wears a white hat that turns him luckier,

and he watches Captain Carpenter stuff two red shells
in, then fold his shotgun straight again. My father

> rocks forward fast with his pole. His cigarette
> is stuck to his lip. Captain Carpenter spits

into the wake and blows a bird's open wing off.
That goddamned seagull's thieving bait

> *that ain't even his,* he says. *Son of a bitch,*
> my father laughs, *we'll catch some fish today.*

My skinny grandfather came to Florida with us,
too. He wants to give his cancer away,

> and nobody else will take it now. He kicks
> a jellyfish back in the water so I won't step

inside it. They act like they're dead sometimes,
but they still know how to sting you. My mother

> came here to get another baby. *Yes, Jim,*
> *I do,* she whispered on the train when I pretended

to be sleeping. When the train stopped at Jacksonville,
an old black man with one leg waved in at me

and I heard Tommy laughing somewhere.
Jimmy wants to kill an alligator here.

One not even big one could make a belt
and shoes and a bag with bumps to carry them,

       like in the Paradise Hotel store,
       where my grandfather bought me a wallet

with both our names on it—BILL.
My grandmother said she wanted a miracle

       but she couldn't find any in that store.
       All the people on the Jungle Queen

paid to see a Seminole village.
They lean over the railing, and they point

       their cameras where the green river swishes.
       My father won't let Jimmy climb over

the round wall to kill the alligator,
so Jimmy throws sand right down on its head.

       The big Seminole boy needs a belt and shoes
       and a shirt for the sun. He wakes the alligator up

with a stick, then tickles him under the chin.
All the white adults have coats and sweaters on.

       The Jungle Queen captain leans his elbows
       on the wall and laughs. His black tie hangs down,

and the boy grabs the alligator's mouth
with both hands and flips it over twice.

       Now he sits on its back and pulls the mouth way up.
       Say ahhh, my father says, and the boy

bends his head inside but the alligator
snaps hard, and the boy's black hair flies up

> as he jumps away. *You see,* my mother
> tells Jimmy, and turns away to buy the doll

with the dress that's orange and black and has white stripes
from the Seminole girl dressed like her doll.

> The boy rubs the alligator's belly
> and it stops moving. I think he killed it.

The palm trees around the Paradise pool
are giant pineapples. Green flies keep landing

> on my father's feet. *Son of a bitch,*
> he says, and swats them off with his paper.

I can hear Tommy singing under the water.
Everyone has a glass with a straw, and green

> cushions on their long, flat lounge chairs. *I'm coming,*
> I answer, and no one sees me talk to myself.

I hold the railing and walk down the wide steps.
I watch the waiters' white shoes slap and stop,

> and hear my mother's laugh disappear as I walk
> under the blue water. I stop and listen for Tommy.

I hold out my hand for him. *Here it is,* I say.
I don't move. His voice is inside the water.

> *All of us here fly with no wings,* I hear him say.
> *I can see you,* he is saying. *Can you see me?*

Take my hand, okay. Hold on. I'll pull you back,
I tell him, but my father is yelling now, pulling me out,

so Tommy can't talk to me anymore.
My mother holds my face and cries. *Stupid*

bastard, my father shouts down at me. *Jesus*
Christ, we didn't come here for this, you know.

New Car Show Season for Jim,
September 1954

After World War II, no dealers had to work to SELL cars—
you just took names. Cash under the table, that was the car business
then, until 1950, when I got in and production caught up. My father
got sick in '47, BEGGED me to help him out. If I didn't have kids,
and if he hadn't cheated me, I'd still be with him. The kind of man
who forgets who raised him, turns his back on his family,

better have just cause. You KNOW I did. And I had my own family
to raise, two kids and a wife who wanted more. I switched to cars
because there wasn't a snowball's chance in hell my old man
could cough up the 40 grand he owed me. His typewriter business
was okay, but he'd gambled away all my commissions. Only kids
like me get STUCK in this guilty shit—only son, help out your father,

you know what I mean? Play the sucker and let your father
bleed you dry's more like it. What the hell, you can't pick the family
you land in, right? Let me tell you, thank God none of your kids
has died. Then you'd . . . Look, you're a great customer. Three cars
in three years, the ten step-vans you got for the delivery business
last year—I'm grateful as HELL, okay. You're my friend. But, man,

when you tell me to stay, with Betty pulling this? What kind of man
hangs around with a NUN? Shit, I liked Howard. I'm sorry her father
died, but it's not my fault. I jumped in to help him with the business
as soon as I could. I didn't marry his daughter to steal the family
jewels, for Christ's sake. I don't need to sell these frigging cars.
I'm a GREAT salesman, with anything. I could support TEN kids

selling pastrami sandwiches in Lent. We get two healthy kids
and then, ka-blam, the roof falls in. I just want to be a decent man,
have kids that aren't screwed up, enough savvy to move cars
out the door, and a REAL WIFE. That's all I want. I'm not my father,
gambling and beating the holy bejesus out of my family
whenever I'm tight. Sure, I whack the boys, but that business

of a leather whip out in the back shed, forget it. And this business
of telling some wiseass PRIEST about it. Just my luck, one of my kids
will get the fucking call. "Don't let your wife turn your family
Catholic"—that's the best advice I could give an unsuspecting man
about to strap on the old ball and chain. Maybe my father
was right. Just beat them up. Christ, who knows . . . These new cars

are SOMETHING, aren't they? I need at least one more salesman,
maybe two, since I caught Tommy Salerno skimming. His wife
owed a big nut, I guess. She was keeping fifteen BINGO cards alive
every game, ten games a night. Her sister Tina's a good customer,
she let me know. But does my guy Salerno ask for help from me?
Not a chance. He rigs up his own greasy little operation—

covers the trade-ins with CASH, ships them up to a two-bit operation
by the Plattsburgh air base, and splits the profits with the salesman
up there. The cars never went on the books. What do they take me
for, stupid AND blind? Jesus, I pay thieves here, I go home to a wife
who won't screw anymore, I listen to tire-kickers and piss-customers
and pipe-smokers all day long. These RPI professors remain alive

just to bust your balls. And to keep ANY shot at a car deal alive,
you have to lay out a four-door Bel Air's entire mechanical operation,
the differential torque at this or that RPM, while ANOTHER customer
walks in, glances once at the sticker price, turns to a salesman—
boom, says, "I'll take it." By this time the pipe-smoker's tight-butt wife
is slamming the driver's seat UP and back, his kids running by me

playing cops and robbers, and he's explaining SPECIFICALLY to me
how many foot-pounds of pull at the axle can keep a car alive
in THIS much snow. By now I'm staring at his cute little wife,
God help me, plotting how I can tell her this automobile operation
is all mine now . . . Hey, I'm the BOSS. I'm not just a car salesman,
and I can take as much time as it takes for a pretty customer,

okay? Letting her see right there I can TELL she'd be a hot customer
while her hubby lectures those college boys. Oh, Christ. Listen to me.
I sound like I'm in some sleazy joke about a door-to-door salesman
you'd hear. I DON'T WANT TO BE THAT. If Tommy were still alive,
and if Howard had survived that second cancer operation,
maybe Betty would have remembered she promised to be my WIFE.

And God damn it, she owes me something if she IS my wife,
RIGHT? The way I stock parts and offer service to a loyal customer
who pays hard-earned money for a new car at my Chevy operation
here. Maybe I'm NUTS, but that certainly sounds right to me,
you know. It's the old drive that keeps a good salesman ALIVE,
and the same goes for a marriage. Go out there, ask any salesman—

ask Mike Spiak or Bill Hogan if a salesman needs a loving wife.
Ask Frank Shortell what keeps HIM alive. Ask any customer
with balls ANYWHERE. Don't trust me. Ask any guy at YOUR operation.

Billy Wakes Up from his Dream and Sees His Brother, David, June 1955

Davy Crockett is driving a silver Fairbanks truck,
but only for tonight. Rounding the curve
on the Hoosick Street hill, near the wide
spot where the boy watched Kevin Ryan's perfect
iceball shatter the bus driver's front window,
Davy spreads his Seminole war chant
over the radio's rhythmic *We're gonna*
rock around the clock tonight, We're gonna
rock rock rock till the broad daylight.
The truck's headlights rake the red, white
and blue WELCOME TO TROY sign, lurch
out of the turn by Franny Clemente's
house and shoot straight down the hill,
silhouetting the boy asleep in his room.
They light up his coiled sock caught
in the glass ceiling lamp, his bunched-up
cowboy sheets with their riderless horses
and empty, colored hats, and his coonskin cap
slung tail-down on the maple headboard
post. They outline the dreaming boy's
worried face. It is snowing hard in his dream.
Kevin Ryan's hands are spiked with glass
shards, but Kevin doesn't care. He is skipping
along the blood-spattered sidewalk,
pumping his right arm down, then up,
then down again, signaling to Davy,
shouting furiously, *Come on, come on,*
until Davy spots him and shouts back,
You heard what the doctor said,
before he delivers three sweet blasts
on his Fairbanks' air horn.
A Freihofer's bakery van is in the way, stuck
at Hoosick and 23rd, and its driver,
in pajamas, wedges hot cross buns under

the back tires. But Davy is waving good-bye
to Kevin, and when he looks back it's too late
to brake or turn. *I'll call the doctor,* he yells,
as his rig jackknifes into the boy's living room.
No, you don't, the boy hears someone say,
and he turns to see the magic light in the hall
that scares away the witches under his bed,
to see his father's naked back hunched
over David's white crib. *Look at his tongue,*
the boy's mother is crying. *Don't let him
swallow his tongue, Jim.* The boy can see
a car's red lights sway and disappear
up the hill outside his window. The streetlight
shimmers in the thin fog. His older brother
is asleep across the room.
Jesus Christ, he won't stop, his father is yelling,
and now the boy slides out of bed to look.
Half of David's mouth is a bent, quiet smile,
and his father's fingers search in the other half
as the boy's little brother jolts back and forth
against the lowered crib bars. David's hands twist
straight down, stretching toward his curled feet.
The boy steps close to see the rolling eyes
trapped underneath a big boy's forehead,
and thinks of Superman's neon head on the pinball
game at Ned Abbot's store. *No, I don't want your
doctor here,* his father says. *It's his goddamn fault.*
His mother's face wants to cry, but she won't
allow it. *It's nobody's fault,* she shouts. *Look
at his head,* his father shouts back. *I TOLD HIM.
This isn't a baby's head. He's eighteen months old,
Betty, and he can't even walk.* When the boy's mother
turns away, she spots him and rushes over.
It's okay, she is saying, *that isn't David's real face.*
She is rubbing his arms, making him too hot.
*That's the mask David wears when he gets sick.
It's not his true face.*

And now the boy can see nothing is really wrong.
This is just a different kind of dream.
His father could be teaching David to swim.
Maybe they're not really in Troy after all.
It could be a Sunday afternoon.
His father doesn't work on Sundays.
The boy will stand in the glassy water. He can smell
steaks popping on the grill, next to his log cabin.
He turns to look up. Davy Crockett will be loading
Old Betsy on the terrace. His grandmother,
setting the porch table, does a double front flip
and waves. A horn blows in the driveway above
the house, and The Millionaire steps out of his car,
draws an envelope from his suit pocket,
checks his watch, and starts toward their steps.
The boy will feel the sun baking his arms.
He'll hear his father's close laughing
as the lake swirls cool around his legs.
He will look down at his right hand,
searching down his long, crosshatched life line,
and will see he has time to change almost
everything.

OUR LADY OF VICTORY   TROY, N. Y.   GRADE I   1955-56

At the Spelling Bee, One Week After the Tonsillectomy, May 1956

Sister Mary Frederic doesn't want me to win. I know it.
                I can tell
            from the words she's picking for me.
              C-H-A-L-L-E-N-G-E.
              U-N-K-N-O-W-N.
              F-A-M-I-L-Y.
Those aren't first-grade words.
                  I saw UNKNOWN and CHALLENGE on Jimmy's
        third-grade spelling sheets.
Sister Mary Frederic wants Jim Berthiaume to win,
                    because he wears glasses like her
      and won't laugh at my jokes
              during class.
            And because I use impure words.
              M-U-T-H-U-R.
I can't believe Paul Cioffi just spelled MOTHER
                      with two *U*'s.
        His ears are really red,
              and he covers them with his hands
     after he sits back down.
                My throat still hurts,
        even when ice cream slides down over
                  where the doctor cut.
My father brought me to Stewart's without Jimmy last night,
            for a make-your-own sundae,
     and the cut-up peanuts scraped worse
                   than the crisp bacon
        at the hospital.
And I have impure thoughts,
      but Sister Mary Frederic didn't talk about those today.
          Can your guardian angel be black?
That's all I asked her, and she threw what
          my mother calls a
                conniption fit.

C-O-N-N-I-P-T-I-O-N. That's how it sounds, anyway,
                              but I never saw it written anywhere.
                Your soul isn't pure white anymore, Billy.
That's what she said back to me, and started to explain all about
                              venial sins
            and mortal sins again.
                                        Small black spots
                and really big black spots,
that's most of the difference, I guess.
                              It's how big they are that counts,
                                    and how much white they cover up
                                    on your soul.
I wanted to ask if Tommy's soul was white when he died,
            but I asked her how big
                                        my soul was instead.
                        She walked away and wouldn't answer.
                              T-A-R-G-I-T.
That's it for Artie DeFillips. He can talk like Daffy Duck,
                and he laughs into his right hand so no one hears.
                        He's smiling now,
            all the way back to his seat.
                              He always says, *Ahh, who cares?*
            I think Artie was just sick of standing up.
                My father told me not to cry
                              when they left the hospital,
him and Mom,
                but that room was too big with all the beds
                        and the white curtains around
            so you couldn't see who was crying
                              or if you knew any other kids,
                        and the sheets were too cold.
                              E-M-T-Y.
If Maureen Connolly wasn't pulling at her underwear,
                                                    like always,
                she could have guessed EMPTY.
            She never gets the silent-letter words, though,
                and when Sister Mary Frederic makes us polka
                        around all the desks,
                              Maureen smells like mayonnaise.
            Peter Keegan is next.

He lives past my grandmother's house, near John Mullins,
whose father is a giant.
K-N-I-F-E-S.
Peter won't sit down.

Hey, Sister Mary Frederic,
that's what you said, KNIFES,
but she rolls up her sleeves so we can see her hairy arms
and says, *Knives, Peter,*
I said knives. Now sit down.
Peter showed me his father's dark tobacco pipes.
He said he smokes them in the afternoon,
after school,
alone, and gets an election.
I told him, *Yeah,* like I understood.
Then I told Peter about ether, and how they had me count
from 100 backwards,
how at 97 a nurse slapped a white cloth on my mouth,
so I kicked and tried to get up
and then my foot hit the doctor
right between the legs
and I saw him kneel down fast
before they made me fall asleep.
Now Jim Berthiaume and I are the only ones left.
H-E-A-V-E-N.
That's Jim Berthiaume's word.

See what I mean? HEAVEN's in our catechism
we read every day. HEAVEN's too easy.
HEAVEN's a snap.
My mother said Tommy was different,
that he got too sick to leave the hospital,
that I wasn't sick that way.
But I was crying,
and she promised three or four times
she'd come back to take me home.
E-A-R-T-H.
I know EARTH from the painted bookcover under my globe.
There's nothing to cry about,
the nurse said.

Lights out at eight in the kids' ward,
and the light from the street outside made

the whole room scary.
The nurse wouldn't take me home,
so I ran away,
down all the stairs with the red EXIT arrows
to the basement.
A-L-L-M-I-G-H-T-Y.
Sister Mary Frederic's mouth is hanging open.
Jim Berthiaume put an extra L
into ALMIGHTY.
And she's going down her spelling list
for one last word
to make me miss, too.
I couldn't find a door out of the hospital basement.
An old black man,
dressed in the same green as all the pipes and windowframes
was singing,

Well, since my baby left me,
I found a new place to dwell—

when he saw me.
His mop was spinning in circles,
cleaning the floor,
but all by itself.
He told me I could come closer and watch,
and his arms weren't moving a bit,
I swear.
Your brother got two wings this long,
he said, and he held his hands apart
this far
to show me how long.
Sister Mary Frederic's finally found a word, and she's smiling.
Here's your final word, Billy,
and she points up at Jesus hanging there on the cross
over the green chalkboard.
C-R-U-C-I-F-Y.
Patti Peck is still mouthing the letters in disbelief,
and John Alberelli smacks his forehead, loud.
Kia Spalding has a pink barrette
in her perfect blonde hair,
and she sits up straight,
hands folded on her desk,

staring at Sister Mary Frederic, ready,
     paying attention just in case I'm wrong.
       You don't need no tonsils,
  that black man said, holding my hand,
           not to talk to God.
    Then he put a Milky Way on my white pillow
      and tucked me in.
        Now you eat that right away,
  he said, pulling the curtain all around my bed.
         Don't wait.
Sister Mary Frederic won't look at me.
     No one is saying a word.
          I am still standing
    with my left hand hidden in my pocket,
       folding and unfolding
     my brown-and-white
        Milky Way wrapper.

BETTY TALKS TO THE BLESSED MOTHER DURING BILLY'S FIRST COMMUNION AT OUR LADY OF VICTORY, NOVEMBER 1957

After Jesus, did Joseph get you pregnant?
Or did you always roll away and whisper, "No."
Sometimes men won't hear "No." I need to ask you this:
when Gabriel announced
that God wanted

you, out of all other women, to have His Son,
what did you feel? You weren't even married yet,
and when you showed up pregnant, what did Joseph do?
I know that Gabriel said,
"With God, nothing

is impossible," but help me to understand.
How could you believe enough to believe
what you had to: that you'd be the mother
of God—though He'd look
like us, become

one of us, suffer, die, and turn
into who He really was—that you would watch
Him die and hold Him that last time,
and that you'd marry a man
who could blame you

for being pregnant? Blame you for letting your Son die,
maybe? Didn't you have one moment of doubt, ever?
But why would you? That's why God made you
different—pure and sinless.
I want to know

what more God could want from me. What more now?
You must speak with Him. What does He want?
He took my one baby back too soon. He gave
me another who'll weigh
down my heart forever.

And now I'm pregnant again. I know I'm not
the only one in pain. The women's voices
crowding up to you must tire you out.
My mother's mother lost
five children herself.

I know my sorrow doesn't make me special.
But I pray to God and nothing good happens.
How can I change all these troubles?
Billy asked me this morning
how he should pray

to God after he swallows his first Host. I almost
said, "Don't, because He won't listen anyway,"
or, "Pray this new baby is healthy and stays
alive," but I said, "Thank Him
for all you have."

I was never good at telling people
exactly how I felt. I never had
brothers or sisters to talk to, just my parents.
After we learned David
had brain damage,

I tried to tell Jim that it was all my fault.
First Tommy, then we both were sick with the mumps
before Florida. It was me, wanting a new baby
too soon. All of it was my fault.
I went to my priest

instead, and wouldn't give Jim what he wanted.
Oh Mary, help me. He isn't really a bad man.

We were friends once. We played bridge. We went
to the movies. We had fun.
He bought me three

charm bracelets like this one but completely full
of gorgeous gold charms from Tiffany's.
Whenever I wear one, someone says, "Isn't
that lovely." I never
have to buy any

jewelry for myself. If he forced me, would that be
a sin against the Sixth Commandment, *Thou
Shalt Not Commit Adultery*, if he's my husband?
I love him. And I think
I wanted it, too.

I warned Jim what would happen, though, and it did.
"I can't stop it," I told him. That would be a sin
against the Fifth Commandment, *Thou Shalt Not Kill*.
Each and every person
is a true image

of God, created to worship Him. Isn't that right?
I can't change that. I said, "No," and Jim wouldn't listen.
Now I need your help. Can you send Gabriel down,
for me? I don't want
to know when. Let him

come at night, when I'm asleep, if that's best.
Like wind pushing too fast through an open window,
couldn't he pass his hand across
my stomach one time, simply
touch me once

and take the baby back? Is that a mortal sin
because I'm asking for it? Mary, I need you.
I know I'm not pure, but show me a sign. Move
a finger. Open up
your eyes for me.

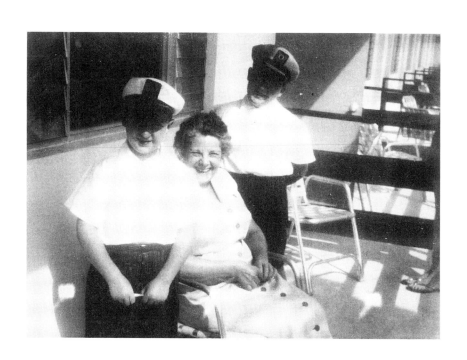

BETTY'S MOTHER WATCHES THE BOYS
IN FORT LAUDERDALE,
MARCH 1958

Dear Mom & Dad,

Hope you are having a good time
in Atlanta with all of your car friends.
Gram told me you are coming back in 3 days,

on Wednesday night, but past
my bedtime. So if you count today in,
the mailman has 4 afternoons to bring you

this letter. Gram let us stay
up until 11 o'clock last night, but not
David. She got David to sleep by 8, then

watched LEAVE IT TO BEAVER
with us. And GUNSMOKE later, after
all those bubble songs with Lawrence Welk.

Jimmy kept his hula hoop
spinning 18 minutes 12 seconds before church
this morning. That was 3 minutes 43 seconds

longer than my fireball lasted.
Gram told me to say a couple of bad things happened
yesterday, but they weren't as bad as the meat fork

I stuck in Jimmy's hand
last Halloween when he ripped my Woody Woodpecker
costume on purpose and made my nose bleed. Remember?

So don't worry. He is okay.
And I went to confession yesterday
afternoon, after they got the elevator opened up.

Gram told me that God was
frowning at me, because of our trick. When I frown
in the mirror, though, my forehead pushes my eyes smaller,

so how when God frowns
could he watch everywhere around the whole earth
to catch any kid who might be acting bad, even in CHINA?

Maybe God has different eyes.
Hey, why did the angel lose his job? Gram
found this joke in the newspaper. Do you give up?

Because he had harp failure.
She said you'd think it was funny, but I don't know.
What do you think? Gram just looked over at me again

and said, *Tell them what happened,*
or no Elvis Presley. Elvis is being joined
into the army in a week, so he can only sing

and shake around once more
on Ed Sullivan tonight. Remember
the arrow with the wire half-circle in the middle

that Dad brought us? Jimmy
snuck it here in his suitcase, and we borrowed
ketchup from a table by the pool right after you left.

We put the arrow around
my head, and Jimmy shook out ketchup to hide
the wire and act like blood, but then the trouble really

started. I pushed the 4 button
in the elevator, and our rooms are on 3. You know
where they are, right? I forgot. Well, Jimmy yelled

at me and punched my arm.
He hits me a lot but that's okay.
He lets me swim and watch TV with him, too.

So then Jimmy slammed
the 3 button when we were still going up
and wham, the elevator stopped. We pushed the doors

open so one finger
could wiggle through and we screamed out into
the dark a long time for somebody to help. I was crying

and Jimmy hollered at me,
You did it, just shut up, and made me keep
the arrow on. It was hot in there, and I lay down

with my head straight so the arrow
didn't poke against the elevator rug, and I fell
asleep. Gram was standing right outside the doors

when the hotel guy pulled
them apart, and she screamed. It was the ketchup-blood,
I think. *I killed him, I killed him,* Jimmy started shouting,

and I kept my eyes closed.
Some of that ketchup stained the rug, Gram said
later on, and then she told me God was not happy

with boys who played tricks.
How does God act when He is happy? I asked,
and Gram didn't answer. She was saying her rosary,

*offering her mental pain
for religious vacations,* she said. Is that when
nuns can go to the beach? How do they go swimming?

Can they take their habits off?
This morning Gram was crying. She had a dream
about skating. Grampa was in his Cadillac, and he drove

her down to a frozen river.
Mr. Parker was cutting out blocks of ice, she said,
and it was all at night with a long stripe of moonlight

so everyone could see.
Horses were watching their white breaths pop out
when they snorted. Gram's father was skating with Grampa,

inside that stripe of moonlight,
but she couldn't catch up, and she woke up crying.
I had a dream that I was a foot taller than Jimmy.

It's time for lunch now.
I have to stop. I promise I will be good,
okay? If the new baby comes out a girl, maybe

she won't fight, or yell
I hate you, like me, and you won't yell back at her.
Gram has called twice. Don't forget to read this. Good-bye.

Love, Billy

Jim Skates Away on Lake George, December 1959

You remember what I whispered to you in the hospital?
                    "You're too TOUGH to die."
Did you hear that? Your right hand twitched once,
                    the hand with the IV taped
between the two darkest liver spots, your right hand
                    you used to shove down
inside your pants pocket for the bicarbonate of soda—
                    "Sweet Jesus," you'd moan
and tap out a white circle of soda crystals from the packet
                    onto your palm, toss
that in your mouth, and grab whatever was close at hand
                    to wash the stuff down.
Sometimes it was water, or milk—sometimes it was scotch.
                    "Rub my back," came next,
then you'd belch, bring up the gas from your rotting gut,
                    get that GAS up and limp away
scowling, like some wounded captain who just learned
                    all his medics got shot.

The kids are playing hockey in front of the boathouse,
                    Dad, and I asked both of them
what they want to be. Jimmy said, "A rich businessman
                    like you," and Billy said,
"I think I'll be a priest." I lost my temper, screaming at him,
                    and he's STILL crying.
Take a look up there, at the camp. Looks like a real house
                    now with the new bedrooms
and the porch all closed in. You never did pay me that
                    40 thousand you owed
for my commissions. Forget about it. I made five times
                    that much last year.
Maybe that 40 grand bought you one perfect moment—
                    a full house or a blackjack
at just the right time, maybe a kiss for Mom you really meant

under some perfect moon
somewhere that washed away all her bruises—a moment
              that came back at the end.

You lugged PAIN around your whole goddamned life, didn't you?
              From your half-foot
that wouldn't heal, to the bleeding ulcers, to the busted
              bile duct. I couldn't say
everything, that last hour waiting in your hospital room,
              but the bastards killed you.
It finally took a bunch of half-assed St. Mary's quacks
              to finish you off.
They nicked a kidney fixing up your ruined bile duct,
              the youngest one said,
and then Martin, a guy I play GOLF with for Christ's sake,
              said, "Jim, you understand, I'm sure,
in a long operation, kidney failure is a common complication."
              But they had a machine,
Dad. They had their brand-new frigging kidney machine
              that swaps good blood for bad.
You didn't need to die. I told Martin, "I want him on THAT,"
              and he said it was booked.
Nothing he'd like better. He was sorry as hell. Machine
              was already scheduled for people
dying, and I screamed at him, "What's my old MAN doing?"
              April 26, 1959. Two days
before my 36th birthday. What kind of present is that?

              I don't remember you
laughing much. Once, last year in Florida, driving down
              to fish for marlin
on Cliff Carpenter's boat, with Billy in the backseat,
              you pushed your '57
Bel Air convertible up over 100 on the long bridge
              that snaked in and out
of that big swamp and all of a sudden you started
              WHOOPING like Cochise
chasing after Custer or somebody and you looked
              over at me, really laughing,
and you winked, you remember? Like I was one of your

drinking buddies.
But it was you, just happy. You hadn't touched a drop yet.

                    At Charlie Mason's funeral home,
where you were laid out, something happened. I know you
                    really didn't give a shit
about my kids. That's okay. Steven was born in August,
                    remember? Just about
nine months before you died. Did you pick that new baby
                    up once? You know damned WELL
you frightened all my kids. Even dead you scared Billy.
                    Betty's mother told him
to go up next to you, kneel down, pray a little, and then kiss
                    your cheek, kiss you good-bye,
I guess. Well, Jesus, Billy knelt there and knelt there, sneaking
                    glances sideways at you,
afraid to budge, then when Anna spoke to him and gave him
                    a little nudge toward YOU,
he jumped up like his clothes were on fire and ran straight out
                    Mason's front door,
out onto 109th Street. He tore up toward Oakwood Cemetery
                    and made it across 6th Avenue,
onto the boulevard strip of grass, before I caught up with him.
                    What the hell, Dad,
the way you beat Mom, the way your eyes looked when you yelled,
                    you figured out how to scare
everybody. At least I learned that—Billy was scared to death
                    when I grabbed him.
Later, in his room, he asked me if I was sad you were dead.
                    "I'm GLAD the son of a bitch
is gone," I said. I don't know if I meant it or not. I don't know.
                    And I don't know how
to get rid of you, either. Everywhere I turn now, you're there.
                    So here's your chance to talk.
Tell me what you NEVER said when you were here.
                    Was there anything I did
you were really proud of, apart from my killing Nazis?
                    Are you where you should be—
I know you hated ice and hated flying—did your hot times
                    in Miami get you ready for it?

I want to know. Tell me. Was your cut-off foot waiting for you?
                    Tell me if you can see
what I'm doing. You hear me? You know what I think?
                    Tell me what God's voice
sounds like, and if He explains all the cruel shit that He does.
                    Have you learned how
to take care of your wife and family over there? Tell me.
                    Tell me money's only money.
Tell me if you have rain and wind and leaves wherever
                    you are. Have you even got
a face for the rain to fall on? Are you part of the wind?
                    Tell me what will happen
to my kids if I skate away like this and keep on going.
                    Tell me if Billy will wave
until I'm out of sight, or skate after me, still crying,
                    and get lost himself.
Tell me why you beat Mom. Tell me why nothing I did
                    was ever GOOD enough for you.
And tell me why, all those years, you never once could
                    say that you loved me.
I don't need all the answers. Today just give me the last one.
                    Forget about the rest.

Last Day at Camp Timlo,
August 15, 1960

Look at this photograph, would you?
What, besides the older, taller boy
smashing the mosquito on his face
makes it unfamiliar?

                                        Nothing, really.
A father smiling with two of his sons,
some cut lengths of softwood stacked low
behind them, a cluster of scattered
pines, trunks straight as thick masts
and limbless before a scrim of foliage,
plus this single-story, nondescript building
and the bulbous, white tip of a propane
tank, like some arctic animal sunbathing
quietly—what else is there to see here?
And look at the shorter boy in the camp
uniform. Why does he look so happy?

                  Tribal council
                        fire
                      dance

His memories swim around in the air
above him, calling down, and he knows
nobody else can hear them.

                  Leather thong
                    ankle bells
           and knotting his feather
                   headband,
            scraping the still-hot
              charcoal sticks
           across Blackfoot face
           and Blackfoot chest.
              Blackfoot scum

Blackfoot scum
the Sioux
boys kept chanting
from the sides.
The boy cut
and John Mullins cut,
and they pressed
their blood
together
into their new
Blackfoot wounds.
Tribal council
fire
dance.
Blackfoot scum
Blackfoot scum.
And John Mullins
pushed out naked
later
by his Cabin 6 brothers
into cold rain
for *jerking off,*
those words the boy
didn't know
before for that,
jerking off
down in the bottom bunk
like they all did,
jerking off
but John Mullins
the one caught
and shoved out naked
into cold dark,
yelling
so long
to get back in.

Prone rifle position? his brother says, laughing,
leafing through the boy's awards. *He's qualified*
as marksman and pro marksman at 50 yards.

Junior bowman, bowman—hey, look out, Dad,
it's Robin Hood of Timlo Forest. His brother's
freckled acne glistens in the August heat.
The boy smells again the camp truck's
canvas roof on each 6 A.M. Sunday trip
to mass in town. He sees the damp choir loft
where his Catholic counselor let him hide
and sleep in the dark before camp day began.

Swimming
with Tony Gorman
under purple war clouds
over Trout Lake,
where the white-bellied
floaters
rocked their dead stares
against the boy's arms
when he swam,
and sliding
in the gathering dusk
through gnat-swarms
and lightning bugs
like Confederate spies,
ducking past
their blind sentries
to capture their bloody flag,
Cabin 7's hairy counselor's
red T-shirt—
and sitting then
with the wind
raking jagged sparks
from the half-dark
ghost-story
fire circle
out over the loud water on
the white-capped lake,
the monster lake,
the dead campers' gleaming
crushed-bones lake.
It's after you now.

It's coming up.
Run,
the counselors yelled,
laughing
as the boys
slipped
and fell
and ran.

The boy doesn't care what his brother says.
He has lived through all of it now.
He knows what his mother sees in her lens.
Not that this father and older brother
look so much alike—white golf
shirts, khaki Bermuda shorts, leather belts—
and are washed smirking toward transparency
by Blackfoot sunlight. She doesn't see that.
She is mounting her new snapshots already,
trying to fix her family in one safe place,
pasting *Last Day at Camp Timlo* next to
Billy in a Camp Canoe under *Billy in Front
of Cabin 6,* working to finish the roll
before they visit Niagara Falls. *A boy
fell out of a boat, you know, went right over
the Falls,* his father is saying. *No life vest,
no nothing. Seven-year-old named
Roger Woodward. Last week. And he lived.*

Roger Woodward,
the boy repeats
over and over
to himself.
Roger Woodward,
he is thinking,
already looking there
at the Falls,
staring up
and tracing
the falling arms and legs
that twist

in erratic circles
like exploding pinwheel fireworks,
spinning diamond-white
and mixing
with the water's
bright
foaming thunder.
Can you see
the boy in the tour-boat's
prow,
right there,
clutching the curved
gothic rail,
the monk's hood
of his dark raincoat
flapping
in the mist?
Can you see him
there now
alone
smiling up,
peering through the angry spray
and watching
Roger Woodward
somersaulting
wild-eyed
down
toward him now?
Come on,
the boy cries out,
come on,
Roger,
I'll catch you.
Roger Woodward,
flying down,
his eyes full of perfect joy
and the glorious terror
of a Great Spirit's
impossible
golden breath

bellowing up from these rocks
and out of this water
cushioning
that boy's
headlong
crazy
fall.

BILLY MAKES A BET WITH JIM, FEBRUARY 1961

Sammy Bizzarro isn't a hockey player, so I don't tell him Manory's
        beat Trojan Hardware
in the 7 A.M. game at RPI this morning, 4-1. I really had a shutout,
        but Michael Gordinier
got a breakaway and smashed into me after his slapshot. We tumbled
        into the goal, and the ref
called it good. *I made the save,* I yelled, but the ref wouldn't listen.
        Sammy doesn't care about
hockey. Plus he's missing *Sky King,* his favorite TV show, to ride
        downtown with me
for *Village of the Damned* at Proctor's, so I let him see my dad's
        Nazi stuff—the Luger,
the flag, and the long knife that has a sideways eagle with wings
        like steps on the handle.
There's no blood on this, Sammy says. *My dad found it after D-Day,*
        I tell him, *in 1944,*
but he's opening my dad's medal cases now. *What's this one for?*
        It's the Silver Star
they gave him for taking out a machine-gun nest single-handed.
        He almost died twice,
once before he even got off the landing craft. Hey, don't point guns.
        Sammy holds the Luger
right up to my nose. His father runs a funeral home on Hill Street,
        and maybe he didn't
fight in WWII or learn about guns to show Sammy how to treat them.
        My dad said it was murder,
where the sailors dropped them, out from the beach in four feet
        of water, and a German,
a Nazi up on the cliffs, had his machine gun trained on the LC's ramp,
        shooting in short bursts
to keep the gun steady and on target. Sammy is reaching back
        into my father's top drawer.
What is THIS? he wants to know. *Wait, let me finish. So every*
        other Ranger in that LC,

jumping up one after the other from the three parallel benches,
          was getting hit, bam,
straight in the chest. Sammy is holding my father's purple toenail,
          the left big toenail
he slammed into the dock at Lake George, with the hole in the center
          that the doctor drilled
to let out all the trapped blood. *The ones who weren't hit had to step*
          on a dead guy's back
to get into the water. And my father couldn't figure out which guy
          would get shot, him
or Syd Ferrar on the middle bench. So then it was time, and Syd
          leaped up, ka-blam,
right in the chest, my dad stepped on his back, and then on the back
          of another guy, floating,
and just like that, he practically ran on top of the water, all the way
          to Omaha Beach.
Sammy is holding the toenail up now, looking through the hole out
          the window, at the snow
starting to fall. *Look at this,* he says, *it works almost like a camera.*

                    *   *   *   *

                    Artie Akullian's sister
                         Janice
          is sitting next to me in Proctor's Theater.
                         Janice is 13, and she definitely needs her bra.
          Artie goes to military school with me and Sammy now,
                    the Albany Academy,
but he hates it, too. Up on the screen,
          a professor is telling his pregnant wife
                         not to worry.
                    You're going to have a baby, that's all, he says.
          It will be a perfect specimen, you'll see.
                         Whose baby? she asks.
               Yours? What sort of life is growing inside of me?
                    Where does it come from?
This movie sucks.
                         All these strange kids in an English village
          get born on the same day,
                    grow up way too fast,

look completely alike,
and hypnotize people when their creepy eyes turn white.
BEWARE OF THIS STARE!
That's what the poster in the lobby said,
but it isn't scary at all,
not like *The Pit and the Pendulum,*
where the steel blade kept swinging
closer and closer and closer.
That was a movie to make out in.
I look over to see if Sammy is watching,
but he and Artie are busy with their popcorn.
I can put my arm around you
if you're scared,
I tell Janice, just in case,
and when the kids stare a villager into blowing
his head off
with his own shotgun,
she buries her face in my arm.
I can smell her hair,
and her Juicy Fruit.
Then Janice takes my hand and pushes it
right inside her blouse,
and stretches up to kiss me.
And not just a kiss either.
She runs her tongue along my bottom lip, too.
So I work my hand down a little,
under the top of her bra cup,
and she doesn't stop me at all.
She's biting my lip now,
and my fingers find her nipple,
which gets tight and hard really fast.
I can hear Sammy and Artie laughing,
they're watching us,
but I don't care anymore.
Janice and I are invisible.
Is there no limit to the power of these children?
someone on the screen says.
No more than there is
a limit to the mind,
I hear the professor answer.

*   *   *   *

In Proctor's men's room, Sammy spots a *National Enquirer* behind a pedestal sink base, and drags it out with his right foot. A boy with tiny hands and a bird's beak for a nose, his wrinkled skin twisting his eyes into burning dots of coal, is smiling on the cover.

PREMATURE SENILITY MAKES 8-YEAR-OLD LOOK EIGHTY!

This kid looks like your brother, Sammy says. *Jesus, look at his head,* I hear him say, but Sammy isn't even talking. He's staring at Kim, their page-five buxom beauty enjoying the sun and a welcome ice-cream cone on Miami Beach—*Hey, what flavor, Kim?*

LOST BIBLE VERSES DISCOVERED INSIDE EGYPTIAN TOMB!

Mom pulled David out of Our Lady of Victory. Sister Mary Frederic couldn't get him to stop his funny noises, so she made him sit alone in the church yesterday, for the whole morning. *I can't believe this,* Mom said. *You can't do that to a child with brain damage. A nun shouldn't do that to anybody.*

**Jesus Christ
returns
to Earth this year!**

**World will end
13 years from now—
in 1974!**

If God created all of us, everyone, why did He make David? What if David was supposed to go to another galaxy and he ended up here? Maybe it was just a mistake, and He's sending Jesus back again to fix all His mistakes. David can't skate, or play hockey. David can't even run, so if Jesus doesn't come back here, what will happen to David then?

IS THIS PHOTO THE PROOF THAT ALIENS LIVE ON EARTH?

*   *   *   *

If you open
the metal door
before
my father's office
on the left
and follow
around
the green
steelplate
spiral stairway
colder than
a snake
to the bottom
and out
through
the curtained
paint bays
down
the spattered
concrete ramp
past the line
of hydraulic lifts
resting their
shiny tubes
in tool-pit
grease
past the used
oil drums
and the bald
tire stacks
you'll see that
behind
the swinging
door
in there
alone

smiling
and ready
inside
John Colarusso's
dark locker
shoving her breasts
tight so only
one nipple can
peek out
against
the Coney Island
Cyclone
entrance rail
stands
Bette Paige.
Bette Paige
oh
yeah
Bette Paige
says
Sammy.

*　　*　　*　　*

Which one is this?
Dolores wants to know, sliding
the special cheeseburger platter
in front of me
and nudging her black skirt against my father's arm.
Billy,
my father says. *Where's his red hair, Jimmy?*
You sure he ain't the milkman's kid?
Nope, I guess he's more his mother's son,
my father answers,
smiling at her.
Here's your patty melt, Dolores says.
Hey, Billy, how's my favorite goalie?
Dominic yells from the kitchen door,
drying his hands on his apron.
We beat Trojan Hardware today,

I yell back. *4 to 1, I heard,* he says.

You get that cheeseburger free.

The Gump Worsley of Manory's Luncheonette.

Jacques Plante, I say back. *Jake the Snake.*

2.54 goals against average last year.

I'm going to play for Montreal someday.

Dominic comes over to our booth now,

and my father shakes his hand.

RPI's got the team this year, Dom.

They murdered

that team from Canada last night.

Nine in a row. Unbeaten. They're first in the East. You believe that?

Fifteen days in a row below zero,

that's what I can believe, Dom says.

You see the paper?

They found a kid from New Jersey frozen up in Congress Park

by the pond, his skates still on him.

Yeah, my father says, *I know.*

Three-quarters of my used cars won't start.

You think I could play for Montreal?

I ask my father. He chews his whole bite of bologna sandwich

before he answers.

I think defense is your position,

he says. *We've got to try you at defense.*

Mike Gregware, Tommy Nelson, Dern Murray—those kids

are in their right positions.

One of them maybe

has a chance, but the NHL is tough, you know.

Dominic is looking away now, retying his apron

as he starts back toward the kitchen.

I'll bet you five dollars

I play for Montreal someday, I say.

I don't know about that, he says,

winking at Dolores.

You won't bet because I'm right,

I yell at him.

No, you're not right. He stands up and pulls

his wallet out of his pants.

You're not right, okay?

He throws a fifty dollar bill on the table.

You want to bet? he says.

I'll bet you this fifty you don't play pro hockey.

He is writing the bet out on his napkin.

Sign this.

We'll keep it in my office safe, he says,

and drops his pen on the table.

I look now to see if Sammy is watching,

but he's busy looking down,

trying to scrape hot meatball sauce

off his white shirtfront with a spoon handle.

Okay, I'll sign it.

I am reaching out for the pen,

and I see again the RPI hockey players last night,

walking toward the locker room after the game.

Can I have your stick?

Can I have your stick?

all us kids were shouting at every player

who went by.

Greg Crozier, John Chiarelli, Ken Astill

who got a hat trick,

and Trevor Kaye, the half-bald one with red hair,

who spit, right at me

when I asked him,

and just kept walking.

It hit the red railing next to my hand.

But then Jim Josephson,

who's the RPI captain,

right behind him,

handed me his, when I didn't even ask for it.

And his stick was almost brand new.

I'm not kidding.

The friction tape on the blade

wasn't even torn.

Betty, Jim & Billy Meet Jayne Mansfield
at the Albany Armory, December 1962

If it weren't for Jim,
there wouldn't be a Cerebral Palsy Telethon.
If it weren't for Jim asking our friends to help,
like Bob Freihofer,
friends with important companies,
or Jim getting the right celebrities here,
like Smilin' Jack Smith and Eileen Woods,
we'd never raise what we need
for a new school at the CP center.
But when Eileen kneels by one of these kids
and sings to him on camera,
or when Smilin' Jack gives his pitch
as they march around with their braces
and crutches or get pushed around
in their wheelchairs,
everyone singing, "Look at us, we're walking,
Look at us, we're talking,"
all the pledge phones light up and stay lit
a long time.
Some idiots always call up and say,
"Oh, you're exploiting those poor kids,"
but the kids love doing it,
being the center of attention.
They think it's a party.

> *Do you believe this Jack Smith slobbering*
> *all over these kids, Bob? He's got this sincere*
> *shtick that everybody buys, though,*
> *so what the hell . . . But Jesus, this Jayne*
> *Mansfield broad, is she the NUTS, or what?*
> *Zibro, Sherry, and Reutemann are dying*
> *for an introduction to her.* "How big a donation
> are we talking, here, boys?" *That's what I*
> *asked them.* "What, are you hogging her?"

they said. "She's got enough for ALL of us."
They're dead right on that, but if anybody's
a high-maintenance skirt, it's her,
you know what I mean? No doubt about it . . .
Like the two broads Eddie and I flew down
to West Palm Beach with after Thanksgiving.
"We've got to be more CAREFUL next time—"
that's what I told him on the way home.

Jayne Mansfield doesn't even look at me.
                    She leans down,
                              she shakes my hand,
       she lets her boobs jiggle around
                                        inside her red dress,
                    she smiles,
                              and she looks right past me.
              She doesn't even see me.
                              And if she did,
                                        what would she see?
                    A 13-year-old in husky pants,
                              that's what.
              But that doesn't matter.
                    She doesn't know anything about me.
                              I'm not a little kid.
       I snuck into the strip tent
                              at the O.C. Buck Carnival
                    last September
       and watched a real blonde do the poison snake dance,
                              and she didn't hide
                              a thing.

We need to find another new school
for David now. He only lasted half a year
at Our Lady of Victory,
where Jimmy went,
and then Billy,
so you'd think with that
and what Jim is for Troy and what he does
for the community,
they'd act a little different.

That nun stuck David in church,
completely alone,
in a cold church pew,
all morning for making noises.
"He has brain damage," *I said to her.*
"Did you think he made them on purpose?"
She had the nerve to say,
"The other children need to concentrate,"
I shot back at her,
"Other children can run and jump at recess.
Maybe they could get used to a few funny noises."
Then I got too angry to say anything else.
So that was that.
I yanked him out of parochial school,
and found a special CP school in New Jersey—
the Walter J. Matheny School
in Peapack-Gladstone,
surrounded by these rolling, wooded hills
and with beautiful horse farms
around every turn.
It's like Jackie Kennedy land down there,
and I can't believe how they treated David.

Eddie and I flew down in his twin-engine,
the Beechcraft. Tina was with Eddie, and
Maureen was with me. They said they had
a house we could use, but the two of them
took us up to this huge goddamn ESTATE—
marble statues, hedges clipped into shapes
like lions and pyramids, whirlpool baths
with dolphin spigots—the fucking WORKS,
you know? And Maureen had this trick
where she'd float her tits on the water
swirling all around us, then hold her breath,
slide under and go at me like an underwater
Hoover, for god's sake. I have no idea how she
could stay under that way, but I thought my
BALLS would pop off once or twice, no kidding.

The strip tent
was the longest tent in the carnival,
with dirty sawdust
and two rows of dark wooden benches
that nobody even sat on.
Men stood and shouted all through
every dance,
until the blonde stripper with giant breasts leaned down
from the stage
and grabbed a man's glasses
right off his face.
She just held onto them for a while,
swinging her pasty tassels in a circle,
but then she slid them still folded
down inside her G-string
and almost everybody stopped yelling.
The music kept on banging away, though.
She was bouncing her hips to the drumbeat,
and a couple of old guys in overalls were clapping,
but it got pretty quiet
until she eased the glasses back out
and held them up to her nose.
When she sniffed the guy's glasses
and made a weird face,
the whole tent exploded into hooting and shouting,
and it made me remember
how Carol Fuller smelled that night last summer
on the bunk in my father's boat, the *Reel Lucky*.
I'm a Methodist. I can't do this,
Carol kept saying,
but she was pushing my hand hard inside her
and then kissing my fingers.
You a real blond, honey?
a man somewhere behind me yelled out,
and then the stripper hauled a poison snake from a basket
and lay down with it on the stage.
Everyone got up on the benches then,
so I snuck down near the front,
just in time to see her arch her back
and wiggle that G-string free.

I wasn't thinking about my parents,
                    or Sister Mary Frederic,
                              or God,
               or anybody who could be angry with me,
                         not when she did that.
          The snake was crawling around on her stomach.
                    Hey, she's a real blond, all right,
                         somebody said,
and those words started to accelerate inside my head
               like the motorcycle on the circular Wall of Death
                    as she hairpinned that snake
                         up and down,
                                   up and down,
                                        up and down.

The first two visits,
once for the interview
and then to bring David down to stay,
Walter and his wife were
all sweetness and light.
Then their complaints began to crop up.
"He's a fussy eater.
He cries too much at bedtime.
He can't even tell time."
And when we went there—
Billy and I would drive down to visit him
at least twice a month—
he looked thinner every single time.
They made him wear a yellow football helmet
all day long in case he fell,
and he looked awful,
like some poor soul
stuck in a foreign refugee camp,
his chin jutting out all pointed and bony.
Then, at the final visit last week,
right out of the blue, Walter says,
"We can't do any more for him.
He doesn't even know what day it is.
Take him home."
I didn't know what to say.

"Good God,
where can he get an education?" *I said.*
"Try Rome State Hospital, up near you,"
he answered,
"they handle the emotionally-disturbed ones."
Jesus.
Emotionally disturbed.
That last trip, a regular swarm of Walter's CP kids
surrounded Billy in their wheelchairs,
grabbing at his arms with their twisted fingers.
He was terrified,
and I don't blame him.
Where were their teachers?
I'm sorry,
but my son doesn't act like that.
We bought David a watch the very next day,
last Monday,
and he can tell time already.

So Sunday morning, we were laying out there
bare-assed on the back lawn—me, Maureen
and Eddie. The sun was hotter than a SON
of a bitch, and it was only about nine A.M.,
when Tina ran out, yelling, "C'mon Eddie,
you gotta get out of here." Ed started laughing,
'cause she'd been yelling at him all WEEKEND
for something, but she really looked scared.
"This is no shit, Eddie," she kept hollering.
Turned out Tina was actually the girlfriend
of Joe Profaci's bodyguard. The Gallo brothers,
who worked for him, led that REVOLT, you
remember? Kidnapped four guys close to him,
whacked two others, and scared Profaci away,
out of his New York place and down to Florida
that MORNING. Only trouble was, we were
laying on the grass at Profaci's Florida place.

I could see the priest's face right through the plastic holes.
Bless me, Father, for I have sinned.
It's been two weeks

since my last confession,
        and these are my sins.
    I've committed an impure act.
     And then I told Father Burke
      about Carol Fuller,
  and about the night on the *Reel Lucky.*
     I knew he'd flip out,
       but when he started screaming,

You're only 13 years old,
    you have hurt and offended the God who loves you,
     staring straight at me through
       the plastic shield,
     I didn't know what to do.
I was thinking how much my grandmother would be hurt
        if she knew.
     He was loud enough the people
   in line outside could hear,
       so finally I got up and left.
I never said the 30 Our Fathers, 30 Hail Marys,
       and sincere Act of Contrition
     he was squawking about.
   Walking home, though, I wondered how
     Father Burke could know
      about my immortal soul?
    What's my soul there for anyway?
     And where is it?
I can't figure out what my soul wants.
      Maybe it has nothing to do with me.
    Maybe it's just here for itself.
   Maybe I should ask Jayne Mansfield where my soul is.
     I bet it's hopping around lost
   inside that red dress of hers.
     Any second now,
she'll reach down in between those perfect boobs,
    lock her dreamy, half-closed eyes on mine,
     and let my soul flap out
       into the world.
     Any second now.

Well, Jim had gotten used to David
not being around,
taking up all my attention.
I know David isn't entirely normal.
I'll grant you that.
But Jim gets so determined to make him
act the right way—
"Even when I'm wrong, I'm right,"
is Jim's favorite saying—
but yelling doesn't work with David.
Jim should understand that by this time.
"Let's try him in Rome,"
he said, and I couldn't help it,
I started shrieking at him,
"Never will I ever allow David to go there."
Jim is so good with money, though.
He'll make this telethon work,
and soon we'll have our own CP school,
but I think bringing Jayne Mansfield here
is absurd.
The men like her, though,
so maybe that will help.
Our friends are certainly donating more this year.
What would she know about children,
especially kids with CP?
She can't even sing well.
If it takes stars like her to build our school,
though, I don't care what she does.
How can anybody watching these kids
not call and give money?
When I see David smile up at Jack Smith
or sing with Eileen Woods,
I really wonder what Jim was thinking.
Rome State Hospital is a warehouse
where you put people
you want to forget about.
He knows that.
I will not have my child there.
Even thinking of it,

having to see David's face as we drove away again,
sends shivers up and down my spine.

Now this week, I'm back in Troy, in my office,
you know, and the PHONE rings. It's Maureen.
"Hey, Maureen, how the hell are you?" *I say,*
and she says back, stiff as my pecker
in the damn whirlpool, "Did you or did you not
take advantage of me on November 28?" *JUST*
like that, I swear . . . So I can't figure out
what, but I can tell something is up,
and I switch my tape recorder on, to be safe.
Then this wiseguy jumps on the line,
calling me this and that and everything.
"You fucked my girl, I'm gonna have your ass,"
blah blah blah blah . . . Well, I'm not blinking,
so he comes up with, "I'm gonna tell your wife,"
and I shoot back, "Be my guest, asshole." *Bingo,*
silence . . . and finally I just hang up on him.
THEN I got nervous, though, and I go to see
Nathan for some legal advice. First thing
he says is, "You want him hit, Jim?" "Christ.
I didn't know YOU could do that," *I say to him.*
"But I don't advise it," *he goes on, sitting back,*
"you buy it once and they'll never let you go."
I'd never pay for that stuff, anyway, Bob.
You know what kind of guy I am, right?
But it showed me something—I guess
Troy's not such a half-assed place, after all.

I wonder if Jayne Mansfield even thinks about
                    ordinary people like us,
          like my parents,
                         and these kids with CP,
                         and me.
               She probably looks at my mother
          answering pledge phones,
     or my father thanking Little League teams
                         for donating milk cartons

they filled up with pennies
and thanks God she's rich and famous
and not like us.
She probably wouldn't even want to go out fishing in the fog
at 6 A.M. on Lake George,
or play gin rummy
at night on our screen porch,
or watch the fireworks my father lights off
on our boathouse roof
every Fourth of July,
or eat my mother's chocolate cake.
She probably doesn't care how much fun we have.
I bet Jayne Mansfield thinks God
keeps His eye just on stars
like her,
that He's disappointed in regular families where kids die
and can't walk right
and people yell at each other a lot.
But if Heaven is there at all
it's pretty high up.
And if God is watching us,
I think we all probably look the same size
down here.
Maybe somebody should tell her that.

Acknowledgments

I wrote the poems that formed the first draft of this book in almost exactly one year, from the end of May 1996 to the beginning of June 1997, while I was part of a three-person poetry workshop. During that year, Tim Cahill, Marea Gordett, and I got together every few weeks to act as editors, encouraging friends, and fellow poets. I have never had a more inspirational workshop experience than that one, and I thank them both for helping me see that these poems could become far better than they were at first.

I am indebted to W. D. Snodgrass, Kathy Snodgrass, and Richard Hoffman for reading early drafts of this manuscript and offering invaluable suggestions. Richard Selzer and Fred Chappell each read the completed manuscript and contributed jacket copy and an Introduction, respectively, for which I am very grateful.

To Steve Huff, Thom Ward, and Robert Blake, my editors and friends at BOA Editions, once more I extend my gratitude for all their efforts for this book, including finding the right title.

I want to thank my partner, Carmel Scalese, for all she has done for me, but especially for her several, essential contributions to various poems in this book and for her tireless readings of whatever I write.

Finally, I thank my parents for the love and loyalty they have shown me, but especially in this context for enduring my recorded interviews with them at different times over the last twenty years, for responding as truthfully as they could to sometimes difficult and painful questions, and for supporting the publication of this book. They have both, in their own ways, answered hardship in their lives with courage and determination.

ABOUT THE AUTHOR

Born in Troy, New York, William B. Patrick has worked in many genres, including poetry, fiction, stage plays, screenplays, and non-fiction. His most recent book of poetry was *These Upraised Hands* (BOA Editions, 1995). *Roxa: Voices of the Culver Family* (BOA, 1989) a novel in prose and poetry, won the 1990 Great Lakes Colleges Association New Writers Award for the best first book of fiction. *Letter to the Ghosts*, Patrick's first book of poems (Ithaca House, 1977) was a finalist for the Elliston Award.

Mr. Patrick spent eighteen months riding with professional firefighters and paramedics in Troy, experiences which culminated in his most recent screenplay, *Fire Ground*, as well as a radio play, *Rescue*, that was commissioned by the BBC and aired world-wide in 1997, and *Saving Troy*, a non-fiction work in progress. He is also the author of a teleplay, *Rachel's Dinner*, which starred Olympia Dukakis and Peter Gerety, and aired nationally on ABC-TV in 1991.

Mr. Patrick has taught creative writing for The New York State Writers' Institute at the State University of New York at Albany, at Old Dominion University, and at Salem State College, among others, and is currently teaching for The Writer's Voice in Silver Bay, New York, and for Alternative Literary Programs (ALPS). He has received grants from the Academy of American Poets, the National Endowment for the Arts, the Massachusetts Artists Foundation, the Virginia Commission for the Arts and, most recently, The New York Foundation for the Arts, to finish *Saving Troy*.

℘

BOA EDITIONS, LTD.

AMERICAN POETS CONTINUUM SERIES

❧